THE GIANT
THE SLINGSHOT
AND THE
FUTURE
KING

BY TAMMAR STEIN

ILLUSTRATED BY DODO MAEDER

APPLES & HONEY PRESS

*To my dear friends Michelle and Riva, who would
lend me their robes and teach me the harp.*
—TS

For all the little brave people.
—DM

Apples & Honey Press
An Imprint of Behrman House Publishers
Millburn, New Jersey 07041
www.applesandhoneypress.com

ISBN 978-1-68115-621-7

Library of Congress Cataloging-in-Publication Data
Names: Stein, Tammar, author. | Maeder, Dodo, illustrator.
Title: The giant, the slingshot, and the future king / by Tammar Stein ; illustrated by Dodo Maeder.
Description: Millburn, New Jersey : Apples & Honey Press, [2023] |
Audience: Ages 6-8. | Audience: Grades 2-3. | Summary: "A story about   bravery, friendship,
and empathy in the early years of the biblical David"— Provided by publisher.
Identifiers: LCCN 2023001055 | ISBN 9781681156217 (hardcover)
Subjects: LCSH: David, King of Israel—Juvenile fiction. | Goliath, (Biblical giant)—Juvenile fiction.
| CYAC: David, King of   Israel—Fiction. | Goliath, (Biblical giant)—Fiction. | Bible. Old   Testament—
History of Biblical events—Fiction. | Conduct of   life—Fiction. | Courage—Fiction.
Classification: LCC PZ7.S821645 Gi 2023 | DDC [Fic]—dc23
LC record available at https://lccn.loc.gov/2023001055

Art direction and design by Elynn Cohen
Edited by Aviva Lucas Gutnick
Printed in the United States

1 3 5 7 9 8 6 4 2

CONTENTS

SHEEP

When David was a boy, he guarded and protected his family's sheep.

Sheep gave the family wool for clothes. Sheep gave the family milk for drinking and for making cheese. Sheep were important, and keeping them safe was very important. But sheep were boring.

David was so bored he tried telling the sheep some jokes. But the sheep didn't laugh. Sheep have no sense of humor.

Then he tried to teach them to play some basic games. But the sheep refused to learn the rules. Sheep can be very stubborn.

To make the days go faster, David learned to play a small harp. He wasn't very good at first. But he had *a lot* of time to practice.

David had a beautiful voice. When he sang, the sheep stopped chewing so they could listen. Sheep do like good music.

At first David played songs his mother had sung to him. Then he played songs he had heard in the village. After some more time, he started playing music no one had heard before. He sang songs that he made up, songs to God.

THE LION

One day, something awful happened.

David was sitting under his favorite tree, playing a new song.

Usually the sheep were quiet when he sang. But that day, in the middle of the best part, they started to bleat. They were scared.

Something was creeping closer and closer to the sheep. It was a lion!

"Go away!" David shouted. Sometimes lions were afraid of loud noises.

Not this time.

"Shoo, shoo!" He waved his hands up and down. Sometimes lions were afraid of sudden movements.

Not this time.

David picked up a rock. He threw it at the lion.

He missed.

The lion grabbed the smallest sheep. Before David could do anything else, the lion and the little sheep were gone.

Oh, the poor sheep! And oh, poor David! His family would be upset that he lost the sheep.

THE SLING

That evening David told his parents what happened.

"That lion will try again," his mother warned him. "We cannot afford to lose any more sheep. You must stop that lion from eating them."

"But this lion is not afraid of loud noises," David said. "This lion is not afraid of sudden motions. And when I threw a rock, I missed."

"Here." David's father handed him a thin loop of leather with a wide pocket in the middle. "This is a sling. It will send the rock farther and faster than anyone can throw it. As soon as you see the lion, use the sling. If you hit the lion, it will run away."

Using the sling was not easy. David had to practice—a lot. Sometimes the rock plopped down at his feet. Sometimes, the rock flew straight up in the air.

Sometimes the rock zigged to the right, and sometimes it zagged to the left.

Sometimes it zipped toward the sheep. Sometimes it zapped right back at him.

David had to be careful not to hit his sheep.

David had to be careful not to hit himself.

It took David a long time before he could use the sling properly. Luckily, he had *a lot* of time on his hands.

THE LION RETURNS

David practiced with his sling every day. Finally, after many months, he could make the rock fly high and far. He could aim and hit a leaf on a tree.

One day, David was relaxing under a tree. He sang one of the sheep's favorite songs, thanking God for making grass and shade.

Suddenly, a sheep bleated. Then another. And another. The sheep were running this way and that way.

The lion was back.

David jumped to his feet. His sling was ready. As soon as he spotted the lion, he grabbed a stone. He whirled the sling around and around.

Out flew the stone. It sailed through the air like a small comet. It landed near the lion's paw, kicking up a puff of dust. The lion stopped, sniffing the air for danger.

Not wasting a moment, David grabbed another stone. He whirled the sling around and around. Out flew the stone. It sailed through the air like an arrow and struck the lion's leg. The lion jumped in surprise and ran away.

The sheep were safe. Hurray for the sheep! And hurray for David! He was able to protect them.

GOLIATH

Several years went by. Then one day, something happened—something terrible.

Two armies had gathered on opposite sides of the valley. On one side were David's people, the Israelites, led by King Saul. On the other side were the Philistines.

The Philistines had a special warrior named Goliath. Goliath was a giant.

He was taller than any man had ever been. He was stronger than any man had ever been. He had never lost a fight.

Every day Goliath walked toward the Israelites and shouted, "Come fight me!"

David's older brothers were part of the Israelite army. They didn't want to fight Goliath. King Saul didn't want to fight Goliath. No one in the whole Israelite army wanted to fight Goliath.

One day, David visited the army to bring his brothers some food. They scolded him.

"If you are here," they asked, "who is watching the sheep?"

David didn't want to talk about sheep. Sheep were boring. He wanted to talk about Goliath. Giants were exciting.

"Someone should fight him," he said. "Why is everyone so afraid?"

"He is a giant," his brothers said. "No one can defeat him."

David disagreed.

"I can," he said.

DAVID AND GOLIATH

King Saul overheard David's words.

"You can't fight a giant," the king said. "You are only a boy. Goliath has been fighting longer than you've been alive."

"When a lion came, I defended my family's sheep," David said. "Now, I will defend my people."

King Saul was impressed with David's bravery.

"You're small, but you're fierce. You don't have armor or even a helmet," the king said. "Here, take mine."

David put on King Saul's armor and metal helmet.

He tried walking. He tripped. The armor was too heavy. The helmet was too big.

"King Saul," David said, "you should keep these." Then he took his walking stick, his sling, and five smooth stones.

When Goliath saw David approach, he laughed. "Ha! You are just a little boy. I will flatten you like a pita. I will squash you like a grape."

Goliath was much taller than David. He was much stronger than David. He was protected by shiny metal armor. His spear was as wide as a small tree. His sword was a long as a branch.

David was short. He was slim. He had no armor. He had no sword or spear.

Uh-oh, David!

THE FIGHT

The two armies gathered in the field to see what would happen.

Goliath's copper armor glittered in the sun. He cast a long shadow. He roared his challenge with a voice that boomed and echoed in the valley.

David had never looked so small or so young. His brothers could hardly bear to watch.

"How are we going to explain this to Mom and Dad?" one of the brothers asked. They all groaned and covered their eyes.

No one believed David could win.

But David wanted to protect the people he loved. He knew he could. After years of practicing, he was very good with his sling.

Goliath stepped forward, each footstep landing like thunder. He raised his sword.

"You can still change your mind!" his brothers called. "Come back!"

But David took off, running toward the giant.

As Goliath continued shouting insults and threats, David took a stone out of his bag and loaded it into his slingshot. David whirled his sling. He let the stone fly.

It hit Goliath right in the middle of his forehead.

The giant fell down with a thud.

Everyone stared. All the Philistines and Israelites were in shock.

The fight between the boy and the giant was over.
The boy had won.

Hurray for David! And hurray for the Israelites!

A FRIEND

After David defeated Goliath with one blow, the Israelites celebrated and cheered. David was a hero!

King Saul insisted that David come live at the royal palace—at once!

David had a fancy room. He ate fancy food. But he didn't like it.

David missed his house. He missed his family. He even missed his sheep.

David was lonely. He felt different from the rest of the people around him. He wore his old, familiar tunic tied with a frayed rope belt and played his harp to pass the time.

One person was friendly to David. It was Jonathan, King Saul's son. He was a prince. One day he would be king. David was only a shepherd.

But Jonathan was kind. Jonathan was funny.

"You need a new outfit," Jonathan said. "You're at the palace now. You're a hero. You need to look the part. Here, take my robe, take my belt."

"Why are you being so nice to me?" David asked.

"Because you're brave, you're loyal to our people, and you're a great musician," Jonathan said. "It's not your fault you have terrible taste in clothes."

David laughed.

"I've been wondering…" Jonathan paused. "Can you teach me how to play the harp?"

David smiled. "I can."

For the first time since he moved to the palace, David wasn't lonely anymore. He had a friend.

KING DAVID

But even with Goliath defeated, the war wasn't over. It was going badly for the Israelites. Eventually, King Saul and his sons—including Jonathan—died in battle.

David's heart was broken when he heard his king and his best friend were both gone.

The Israelites were sad too. They went to David. "You must be our new king," they told him.

David was scared. He felt lost. But Jonathan would have wanted him to try. David had to become the leader of the Israelites. He had to become their king—the king of Israel.

David prayed to God, gathered his thoughts, and decided to answer his people's call.

It wasn't easy. It wasn't quick. But after many more hard fights, the Israelites finally won the war against the Philistines.

After being a lonely shepherd and spending years singing only to his sheep, King David now sang his beautiful songs to thousands of people. He wrote poems that thanked and praised God, as well as ones about being a shepherd. Because as it turned out, you could learn a lot about life from sheep.

Many years later, King David settled in a city on a
hill and made it the capital. He named it Jerusalem.
He designed a huge temple to honor God.

David's life was full of miracles, mistakes, good choices, bad choices, hard work, and amazing achievements.

King David was an old man when he died. His son Solomon became the new king.

King Solomon had many adventures as well… but that's a story for another time.

MORE ABOUT DAVID

Archaeologists and scholars believe that King David ruled from around 1000 to 962 BCE, though the exact dates remain unknown. Ancient stones known as the Tel Dan Stele have been found in northern Israel with inscriptions that mention "the house of David." This is the first archaeological proof of King David's reign as a real historical figure. He is credited with establishing the Kingdom of Judah and its capital city of Jerusalem.

King David is also credited with composing some of the most powerful psalms—sacred poems or songs—which people all over the world still recite. The most famous of them is Psalm 23:

The Lord is my shepherd, I shall not want. . . .

Though I walk through the valley of the shadow of death, I will fear no evil, for You are with me.

DEAR READER

It's not easy starting something new. When we're beginners, everything is hard, whether we're learning to play a musical instrument, trying a new sport, or learning to read. It's easy to look around at other people and think, *"They're so good at this and I'm so bad. Why even bother?"*

But it turns out there's a secret to becoming really good at anything . . . are you ready for it?

Practice!

I bet you were hoping I'd say something quicker, easier, and more exciting. Sorry, I wish I had better news. But if you think about it, practice is kind of magical. Just by trying something over and over again, you get better at it.

David practiced for years with his harp and his sling before he was able to make a difference in the world.

Be patient, be persistent, and keep practicing!